Java Exams Study Guide

David Mayer

2020-12-10

Index

HOW TO GET A 50% DISCOUNT **3**

INTRODUCTION **4**

COPYRIGHT **8**

DEDICATION **9**

ACKNOWLEDGMENTS **10**

PREFACE **11**

HOW TO USE THIS BOOK **12**

JAVA EXAMS **13**

    Chapter 1: 1Z0-803 - Java SE 7 Programmer I 15
    Exam Guide *15*
    Sample Practice Test for 1Z0-803 .... *16*
    Chapter 2: 1Z0-804 - Java SE 7 Programmer II 26
    Exam Guide *26*
    Sample Practice Test for 1Z0-804 .... *27*
    Chapter 3: 1Z0-808 - Java SE 8 Programmer I 40
    Exam Guide *40*
    Sample Practice Test for 1Z0-808 .... *45*
    Chapter 4: 1Z0-809 - Java SE 8 Programmer II 54
    Exam Guide *54*
    Sample Practice Test for 1Z0-809 .... *59*
    Chapter 5: 1Z0-813 - Upgrade to Java SE 8 OCP 69
    Exam Guide *69*
    Sample Practice Test for 1Z0-813 .... *72*
    Chapter 6: 1Z0-815 - Java SE 11 Programmer I 82
    Exam Guide *82*
    Sample Practice Test for 1Z0-815 .... *90*

SUMMARY **102**

ABOUT THE AUTHOR.. 103

APPENDIX.. 104

How to Get a 50% Discount

If you have come this far and are curious about how to get a unique offer, then you surely understand it is essential for you to take the right Java Certification now. There is no more time to waste; it's time to be certified in the right way according to your skills.

By purchasing this book you will then be entitled to an incredible 50% discount code on all products available at www.Certification-questions.com

It is a unique offer, and you will finally be able to understand which is the Certification required for your career, understand how to take the Exam and what are the prerequisites. Also, you will be able to use the only Simulated Exam that always has the latest questions available with 100% guaranteed success and a money back guarantee policy.

Don't wait, send us a copy to info@Certification-questions.com:

- of your book
- of your purchase receipt

And, we will automatically send you a discount code equal to 50% for the best Exam Simulator available on the market.

Thanks - Certification-questions.com

Introduction

Nowadays, finding good work is more difficult than ever; competition is high and skills become an essential factor to check when hiring somebody. For this reason, assuring companies that they have the right people with the right certified skills and knowledge, through Certifications, qualifications and degrees, is the best way of opening the doors to the world of work.

Java Certifications are not to be underestimated.

Java Certification, for those who are not aware of it, is an official document that enables a professional to show their certified skills and knowledge.

A Java certification is highly related to the computer industry and gives a Java developer worldwide recognition. It helps you to find a better job, get a much better salary, and even a much better raise or benefit for your current job. Java is fast, secure, reliable, and free to download. Java runs on JRE with basic JVM support. Java is an object-oriented language with advanced and simplified attributes. Java can work on all systems with some implementation conditions.

If you are just starting out as a Java programmer, so much the better; the benefit of having Java certification right now could be very good. Obtaining Java certifications will surely be helping in position yourself with the approval of having the full set of skills and knowledge to be a specialized Java programmer. Increase your confidence in your command of Java technology. Get more validity, help yourself do much better in your daily work, and lead your group and organization. Capable of creating a robust and feature-rich interface (UI) and eliminates the need for coordinated initiative with professionals and web designers. Not only this, but it also expands your range of skills, but it can also offer you a higher offer than others in the expert market and offers many job opportunities. There are four types of certification degrees organized as part of the Oracle Java certification path. They are:

- Oracle Certified Associate (OCA)
- Oracle Certified Professional (OCP)
- Oracle Certified Expert (OCE)
- Oracle Certified Master (OCM)

In order to understand and productively complete Java certification exams, a satisfactory level of understanding of Java progress is required. You would definitely also need to recognize the test structure, the survey templates to check and acquire the correct technique. This is why hundreds of Java programmers try to get a license every year, but passing this exam is difficult. You need a deep understanding of the Java language and API to pass the exam. With regards to OCPJP, this turns out to be much more crucial as you need to focus on the information to recognize each encryption request before choosing. Although most Java specialists learn as they earn, without going to college or getting expert certifications, some companies appreciate the qualifications.

Many Java specialists gain valuable experience working on projects in a variety of industries, indicating that they are new to the needs of various industries, as well as to the way they deal with designers. While some companies may value their employees more if they have a Java certification as it is beneficial to the company, some companies may simply appreciate the variety of years of experience a Java expert has. That said, having a Java certification on your skills profile certainly doesn't reduce your chances of getting a job.

By adding a Java Certification to your resume, you can make a real difference to your employability and get hired faster because it is proven that Java Certification has allowed human resources to fill job vacancies quickly and in a secure way.

The Exam is both theoretical and practical and consists of multiple choice questions.

The Java Certified Expert is designed for professionals; it is an official document recognized all over the world and aimed at expert users who, upon passing the Exam, will be able to propose themselves as an experienced and qualified specialist of one or more Java programs. The Exam is theoretical and is carried out on an English language platform. The Java OCA program is much more challenging than the OCP program and requires a lot of effort and proper preparation. Therefore, it is good to study and practice as much as possible when trying for OCA Certification.

The Java OCA does not provide actual Certifications but instead offers qualifications, which are obtained from time to time bypassing the OCP Exam together with the Oracle Certified Master Qualification Exam.

This guide provides all the information you need to easily pass Java Exams. Whether you are a beginner or an expert, our team will provide you with everything you need to start studying in detail.

In this guide we will offer you step by step information on the following topics:

- Java Certification Exam registration procedure
- Java Certification Exam topics
- Benefits of obtaining a Java Certification
- Requirements for Java Certification Exams

- The Certification path describes the knowledge of the technologies and related skills necessary to pass the Exams
- Duration of the Exam
- Exam format
- Certified professional salary in different countries
- Price of Java Certification Exams
- Practical tests
- How to obtain the Certification that best suits your professional growth
- 50% discount on the purchase of the Web And Mobile Simulator available at www.Certification-questions.com
- 100% success guarantee

The guide contains everything you need to prepare for the official Java Exams, and to master the skills needed to obtain the Certification that best suits your career path.

In addition to that, we will also provide you with everything you need for making the right decision when choosing a Java Certification: The material in this guide helps professionals to choose the right Certification and to improve their knowledge to pass the official Certification Exam quickly and easily. Our team already provides selected and targeted questions \ answer content to consolidate professional preparation through practical tests and training material.

Our guide provides 100% Exam information, ensuring your preparation is solid and detailed. Thanks to this guide, you will obtain all the necessary information for choosing and passing the Certification that best suits your needs within the huge Java Certification Program.

Copyright

PUBLISHED BY

certificaton-questions.com

Copyright @ 2019 Certification Questions

All rights reserved. No part of the contents in this may be reproduced or transmitted in form by any means (electronic, photocopying, recording, or otherwise) without prior written permission of the publisher.

First Edition

This book is provided to expresses the author's views and opinions. The views and opinions expressed in this book including URLs and other Internet websites referenced may change without notice.

Any trademarks, service marks, product names or named features in this book are assumed to the property of their respective owners and are used only for reference. There is no implied endorsement if the author references one of these terms, logos, or trademarks.

Some examples given are provided for illustration and learning purposes, and are fictitious. No real association or connection is intended or inferred.

Dedication

Do you know how?

You choose a book then go to the Dedication Page and find that once again the author has dedicated a book to someone else and not to you.

Not this time.

This book is dedicated to the readers, as, without you, there would be no need for this book to have been written.

Hopefully the effort put into producing this resource guide will result in value and success when you sit your certification exam.

This one's for you. Thanks - Certification-questions.com

Acknowledgments

The world is better, thanks to people who want to develop and guide others. What makes it even better are the people who share the gift of their time to guide future leaders. Thank you to all who strive to grow and help others to grow.

Without the experience and support of my colleagues and team at Certification-questions.com, this book would not exist. You have given me the opportunity to lead a great group of people to become a leader of great leaders. It is a blessed place. Thanks to the Certification-questions.com team.

I want to say thank you to everyone who ever said anything positive to me or taught me something. It was your kind words and actions over the years that drove me to help others in my turn. THANK YOU.

PREFACE

Are you looking for valid Practice Tests for Java Certification?

This book will guide on how you can pass the Java Certification Exam using Practice Tests.

We will cover a large set of information for Java Certification topics, so you will systemically discover how to pass the Certification exam.

This book will also explore many of your questions, such as:

- Java Exam topics
- What are the essential criteria for passing the Official Java Exam?
- How much Java Exam Cost?
- What is the format of the Java Exam?
- The advantage of Java Exam Certification
- What are the difficulties of Java Exam Certification?

We appreciate you taking the time to read this book, and we are really excited to assist you on your career growth journey.

How to Use This Book

There are four main components to the present Java Study Guide.

First, the Introduction, in which you will get to know about the importance of Java Certification and Practice Tests.

Secondly, the Table of Contents proves quite helpful for maneuvering through the ebook.

Thirdly, there is the Content, in which you will get to know about the different methods of studying for the Java Certification Exam that will help you to pass the Certification Exam on your first attempt.

Fourthly, the Summary, in which you will read the brief statement or account of the main points of the Java Certification Exam.

Java Exams

Java Certified Professionals form a unique community with Java as its hub. Individuals can take advantage of the networking and professional growth opportunities which according to the research is a much more poignant aspect of the value of certification that was previously envisioned. Java also recognizes that the community is an important way to engage with its customer base.

The **Certification-questions.com team** has worked directly with industry experts to provide you with the actual questions and answers from **the latest versions of the Java exam**. Practice questions are proven to be the most effectively way of preparing for certification exams.

Java certified professionals are certified individuals who specialize in Java information technology programs and applications. Experts in the field of Java programs, they focus their technical support skills in various areas, ranging from operating systems, cloud solutions to Web development.

With a certificate, your value increases when you apply for jobs. According to Java your chances of getting **hired increases 5 times**. According to Java, **86% of hiring managers indicate that they prefer job applicants having an IT certificate**. And Java certification is a preference over some unknown computer training institutes' certificates. Eight out of ten Hiring Managers wish to verify the certificates provided by job applicants. Further, according to Java, 64% of IT managers prefer Java certificates to other certificates. Certification, training, and experience are the three main areas that provide better recognition to a person when it comes to promotions and incentives.

We offers an online service that allows students to study through tests questions. The Simulator is built to reflect the final exam structure: It is an excellent study material as it offers the ability to run an online actual exam. Every question is also associated with the solution and each solution is explained in detail.

Chapter 1: 1Z0-803 - Java SE 7 Programmer I

Exam Guide

Oracle Java SE 7 Programmer I Study 1Z0-803 Exam:

Java 1Z0-803 Free Test is a test created to demonstrate all the features of our **Java7 Associate Web Simulator.** You will be able to access 25 complete questions and will have 53 minutes to finish the test.

There are several components you can interact with when you take our **mock exams:**

- Take a look at the progress bar at the top; it will tell how you are progressing throughout the exam.
- Read the question and select only the answer(s) you think are correct by checking the corresponding check box.
- Navigate the **Java Certification Questions** using the "Previous" and "Next" buttons.
- Mark the **Java Certification Questions** you wish to review later. All the questions you have marked will be listed in the right section "marked questions". You will be able to jump directly to the question from this list.
- if you want to take a look at the correct answers for a question, just click the **Solution** button. In the solution section you will be able to check your answers as well as find a full explanation.

- Keep an eye on the **countdown**. This will tell you how much time is left. When the countdown expires, the test will be automatically submitted.
- Once the test is submitted, the **result** section will expand. Here, you will be able to review all the **questions of the test**. From here, you can also navigate directly to each question.

More Info for 1Z0-803 Exam:

For more info visit: Oracle Java8 1Z0-803 Exam Reference

Sample Practice Test for 1Z0-803

Question: 1 *One Answer Is Right*

Given the code fragment:

```
int[][] array2D = { {0,1,2}, {3,4,5,6} };

System.out.print(array2D[0].length + " ");
System.out.print(array2D[1].getClass().isArray() + " ");
System.out.println(array2D[0][1]);
```

What is the result?

Answers:

A) 3 false 1

B) 2 true 3

C) 2 false 3

D) 3 true 1

E) 3 false 3

F) 2 true 1

G) 2 false 1

Solution: D

Explanation:

Explanation: The length of the element with index 0, {0, 1, 2}, is 3. Output: 3 The element with index 1, {3, 4, 5, 6}, is of type array. Output: true The element with index 0, {0, 1, 2} has the element with index 1: 1. Output: 1

Question: 2 *One Answer Is Right*

Given:

```
public class ScopeTest {
    int z;
    public static void main(String[] args) {
        ScopeTest myScope = new ScopeTest();
        int z = 6;
        System.out.println(z);
        myScope.doStuff();
        System.out.println(z);
        System.out.println(myScope.z);
    }
    void doStuff() {
        int z = 5;
        doStuff2();
        System.out.println(z);
    }
    void doStuff2() {
        z = 4;
    }
}
```

What is the result?

Answers:

A) 6 5 6 4

B) 6 5 5 4

C) 6 5 6 6

D) 6 5 6 5

Solution: A

Explanation:

Explanation: Within main z is assigned 6. z is printed. Output: 6 Within doStuff z is assigned 5.DoStuff2 locally sets z to 4 (but MyScope.z is set to 4), but in Dostuff z is still 5. z is printed. Output: 5 Again z is printed within main (with local z set to 6). Output: 6 Finally MyScope.z is printed. MyScope.z has been set to 4 within doStuff2(). Output: 4

Question: 3 *One Answer Is Right*

An unchecked exception occurs in a method dosomething() Should other code be added in the dosomething() method for it to compile and execute?

Answers:

A) The Exception must be caught

B) The Exception must be declared to be thrown.

C) The Exception must be caught or declared to be thrown.

D) No other code needs to be added.

Solution: D

Explanation:

Explanation: Because the Java programming language does not require methods to catch or to specify unchecked exceptions (RuntimeException, Error, and their subclasses), programmers may be tempted to write code that throws only unchecked exceptions or to make all their exception subclasses inherit from RuntimeException. Both of these shortcuts allow programmers to write code without bothering with compiler errors and without bothering to specify or to catch any exceptions. Although this may seem convenient to the programmer, it sidesteps the intent of the catch or specify requirement and can cause problems for others using your classes.

Question: 4 *One Answer Is Right*

Given the code fragment: interface SampleClosable { public void close () throws java.io.IOException; } Which three implementations are valid?

```
A)  public class Test implements SampleCloseable {
        public void close() throws java.io.IOException {
            // do something
        }
    }

B)  public class Test implements SampleCloseable {
        public void close() throws Exception {
            // do something
        }
    }

C)  public class Test implements SampleCloseable {
        public void close() throws java.io.FileNotFounrException {
            // do something
        }
    }

D)  public class Test extends SampleCloseable {
        public void close() throws java.io.IOException {
            // do something
        }
    }

E)  public class Test implements SampleCloseable {
        public void close() {
            // do something
        }
    }
```

Answers:

A) Option A

B) Option B

C) Option C

D) Option D

E) Option E

Solution: A, C, E

Explanation:

Explanation: A: Throwing the same exception is fine. C: Using a subclass of java.io.IOException (here java.io.FileNotFoundException) is fine E: Not using a throw clause is fine. Incorrect answers: B: Exception is not a subclass of java.io.IOException and cannot be used here. D: Not extends. SampleCloseable cannot be the superclass of Test, a superclass must be a class. (An interface extends other interfaces.)

Question: 5 *One Answer Is Right*

Given the code fragment:

```
Int [] [] array = {{0}, {0, 1}, {0, 2, 4}, {0, 3, 6, 9}, {0, 4, 8, 12, 16}};
Systemout.println(array [4] [1]);
System.out.println (array) [1] [4]);
```

What is the result?

Answers:

A) 4 Null

B) Null 4

C) An IllegalArgumentException is thrown at run time

D) 4 An ArrayIndexOutOfBoundException is thrown at run time

Solution: D

Explanation:

Explanation: The first println statement, System.out.println(array [4][1]);, works fine. It selects the element/array with index 4, {0, 4, 8, 12, 16}, and from this array it selects the element with index 1, 4. Output: 4 The second println statement, System.out.println(array) [1][4]);, fails. It selects the array/element with index 1, {0, 1}, and from this array it try to select the element with index 4. This causes an exception. Output: 4 Exception in thread "main" java.lang.ArrayIndexOutOfBoundsException: 4

Question: 6 *One Answer Is Right*

View the exhibit:

```java
public class Student {
    public String name = "";
    public int age = 0;
    public String major = "Undeclared";
    public boolean fulltime = true;

    public void display(){
        System.out.println("Name: " + name + " Major: " + major);
    }

    public boolean isFulltime(){
        return fulltime;
    }
}
```

Given:

```java
public class TestStudent {

    public static void main(String[] args) {
        Student bob = new Student();
        Student jian = new Student();

        bob.name = "Bob";
        bob.age = 19;
        jian = bob;
        jian.name = "Jian";
        System.out.println("Bob's Name: " + bob.name);
    }
}
```

What is the result when this program is executed?

Answers:

A) Bob's Name: Bob

B) Bob's Name: Jian

C) Nothing prints

D) Bob's name

Solution: B

Explanation:

Explanation: After the statement jian = bob; the jian will reference the same object as bob.

Question: 7 *One Answer Is Right*

Given the code fragment:

```
String valid = "true";
if (valid) System.out.println("valid");
else       System.out.println("not valid");
```

What is the result?

Answers:

A) Valid

B) Not valid

C) Compilation fails

D) An IllegalArgumentException is thrown at run time

Solution: C

Explanation:

Explanation: In segment 'if (valid)' valid must be of type boolean, but it is a string. This makes the compilation fail.

Question: 8 *One Answer Is Right*

Which two are valid instantiations and initializations of a multi dimensional array?

```
A)   int[][] array2D = { {0,1,2,4}, {5,6} };

B)   int[][] array2D = new int [][2];
     array2D[0][0] = 1;
     array2D[0][1] = 2;
     array2D[1][0] = 3;
     array2D[1][1] = 4;

C)   int[][][] array3D = { {0,1}, {2,3}, {4,5} };

D)   int[] array = {0,1};
     int[][][] array3D = new int[2][2][2];
     array3D[0][0] = array;
     array3D[0][1] = array;
     array3D[1][0] = array;
     array3D[1][1] = array;

E) int[][] array2D = { 0,1 }
```

Answers:

A) Option A

B) Option B

C) Option C

D) Option D

E) Option E

Solution: A, D

Question: 9 *One Answer Is Right*

Given the code fragment:

```
int b = 4;
b--;
System.out.println(--b);
System.out.println(b);
```

What is the result?

Answers:

A) 2 2

B) 1 2

C) 3 2

D) 3 3

Solution: A

Explanation:

Explanation: Variable b is set to 4. Variable b is decreased to 3. Variable b is decreased to 2 and then printed. Output: 2 Variable b is printed. Output: 2

Question: 10 *One Answer Is Right*

Given:

```java
public class DoCompare1 {
    public static void main(String[] args) {
        String[] table = {"aa", "bb", "cc"};
        for (String ss: table) {
            int ii = 0;
            while(ii < table.length) {
                System.out.println(ss + ", " + ii);
                ii++;
            }
        }
    }
}
```

How many times is 2 printed as a part of the output?

Answers:

A) Zero

B) Once

C) Twice

D) Thrice

E) Compilation fails.

Solution: A

Chapter 2: 1Z0-804 - Java SE 7 Programmer II

Exam Guide

Oracle Java SE 7 Programmer II Study 1Z0-804 Exam:

Java 1Z0-804 Free Test is a test created to demonstrate all the features of our **Java7 Associate Web Simulator.** You will be able to access 25 complete questions and will have 53 minutes to finish the test.

There are several components you can interact with when you take our **mock exams:**

- Take a look at the progress bar at the top; it will tell how you are progressing throughout the exam.
- Read the question and select only the answer(s) you think are correct by checking the corresponding check box.
- Navigate the **Java Certification Questions** using the "Previous" and "Next" buttons.
- Mark the **Java Certification Questions** you wish to review later. All the questions you have marked will be listed in the right section "marked questions". You will be able to jump directly to the question from this list.
- if you want to take a look at the correct answers for a question, just click the **"Solution"** button. In the solution section you will be able to check your answers as well as find a full explanation.

- Keep an eye on the **countdown**. This will tell you how much time is left. When the countdown expires, the test will be automatically submitted.
- Once the test is submitted, the **result** section will expand. Here, you will be able to review all the **questions of the test**. From here, you can also navigate directly to each question.

More info for 1Z0-804 Exam:

For more info visit: Oracle Java8 1Z0-804 Exam Reference

Sample Practice Test for 1Z0-804

Question: 1 *One Answer Is Right*

Given:

```java
class A {
    int a = 5;
    String doA() { return "a1 "; }
    protected static String doA2 () { return "a2 "; }
}

class B extends A {
    int a = 7;
    String doA() { return "b1 "; }
    public static String doA2() { return "b2 "; }

    void go() {
        A myA = new B();
        System.out.print(myA.doA() + myA.doA2() + myA.a);
    }

    public static void main (String[] args) {
        new B().go();
    }
}
```

Which three values will appear in the output?

Answers:

A) 5

B) 7

C) a1

D) a2

E) b1

F) b2

Solution: A, D, E

Explanation:

Explanation: Static method of base class is invoked >> A myA = new B(); System.out.print(myA.doA() + myA.doA2() + myA.a); class B String doA() { return "b1 "; } class A protected static String doA2 () { return "a2 "; } class B int a = 7;

Question: 2 *One Answer Is Right*

Given:

```java
class Product {
    private int id;
    public Product (int id) {
      this.id = id;
    }
    public int hashCode() {
      return id + 42;
    }
    public boolean equals (Object obj) {
      return (this == obj) ? true : super.equals(obj);
    }
}

public class WareHouse {
    public static void main(String[] args) {
      Product p1 = new Product(10);
      Product p2 = new Product(10);
      Product p3 = new Product(20);
      System.out.print(p1.equals(p2) + " ");
      System.out.print(p1.equals(p3) );
    }
}
```
What is the result?

Answers:

A) false false

B) true false

C) true true

D) Compilation fails

E) An exception is thrown at runtime

Solution: A

Explanation:

Explanation: (this == obj) is the object implementation of equals() and therefore FALSE, if the reference points to various objects and then the super.equals() is invoked, the object method equals() what still result in FALSE better override of equals() is to compare the attributes like: public boolean equals (Object obj) { if (obj != null){ Product p = (Product)obj; return this.id == p.id; } return false; }

Question: 3 *One Answer Is Right*

Given:

```java
interface Rideable {
    String ride() ;
}
class Horse implements Rideable {
    String ride() { return "cantering "; }
}

class Icelandic extends Horse {
    String ride() { return "tolting "; }
}

public class Test1 {
    public static void main(String[] args) {

        Rideable r1 = new Icelandic();
        Rideable r2 = new Horse();
        Horse h1 = new Icelandic();

        System.out.println(r1.ride() + r2.ride() + h1.ride());

    }
}
```

What is the result?

Answers:

A) tolting cantering tolting

B) cantering cantering cantering

C) compilation fails

D) an exception is thrown at runtime

Solution: C

Explanation:

Explanation: Compiler says: Cannot reduce the visibility of the inherited method from Rideable. mã¼ssen PUBLIC sein public String ride() { return "cantering "; } public String ride() { return "tolting "; } if this is given then the result would be: A : tolting cantering tolting

Question: 4 *One Answer Is Right*

Given these facts about Java types in an application: - Type x is a template for other types in the application. - Type x implements dostuff (). - Type x declares, but does NOT implement doit(). - Type y declares doOther() . Which three are true?

Answers:

A) Type y must be an interface.

B) Type x must be an abstract class.

C) Type y must be an abstract class.

D) Type x could implement or extend from Type y.

E) Type x could be an abstract class or an interface.

F) Type y could be an abstract class or an interface.

Solution: B, D, F

Explanation:

Explanation: Unlike interfaces, abstract classes can contain fields that are not static and final, and they can contain implemented methods. Such abstract classes are similar to interfaces, except that they provide a partial implementation, leaving it to subclasses to complete the implementation. If an abstract class contains only abstract method declarations, it should be declared as an interface instead. Note: An interface in the Java programming language is an abstract type that is used to specify an interface (in the generic sense of the term) that classes must implement. Interfaces are declared using the interface keyword, and may only contain method signature and constant declarations (variable declarations that are declared to be both static and final). An interface may never contain method definitions. Note 2: an abstract class is a class that is declared abstract--it may or may not include abstract methods. Abstract classes cannot be instantiated, but they can be subclassed. An abstract method is a method that is declared without an implementation (without braces, and followed by a semicolon)

Question: 5 *One Answer Is Right*

Given:
```java
public abstract class Account {
   abstract void deposit (double amt);
   public abstract Boolean withdraw (double amt);
}

public class CheckingAccount extends Account {

}
```
What two changes, made independently, will enable the code to compile?

Answers:

A) Change the signature of Account to: public class Account.

B) Change the signature of CheckingAccount to: public abstract CheckingAccount

C) Implement private methods for deposit and withdraw in CheckingAccount.

D) Implement public methods for deposit and withdraw in CheckingAccount.

E) Change Signature of checkingAccount to: CheckingAccount implements Account.

F) Make Account an interface.

Solution: B, D

Explanation:

Explanation: Compiler say: - Der Typ CheckingAccount muss die Ã¼bernommene abstrakte Methode Account.deposit(double) implementieren - Der Typ CheckingAccount muss die Ã¼bernommene abstrakte Methode Account.withdraw(double) implementieren ODER Typ CheckingAccount als abstract definieren

Question: 6 *One Answer Is Right*

Which two forms of abstraction can a programmer use in Java?

Answers:

A) enums

B) interfaces

C) primitives

D) abstract classes

E) concrete classes

F) primitive wrappers

Solution: B, D

Explanation:

Explanation: When To Use Interfaces An interface allows somebody to start from scratch to implement your interface or implement your interface in some other code whose original or primary purpose was quite different from your interface. To them, your interface is only incidental, something that have to add on to the their code to be able to use your package. The disadvantage is every method in the interface must be public. You might not want to expose everything. *When To Use Abstract classes An abstract class, in contrast, provides more structure. It usually defines some default implementations and provides some tools useful for a full implementation. The catch is, code using it must use your class as the base. That may be highly inconvenient if the other programmers wanting to use your package have already developed their own class hierarchy independently. In Java, a class can inherit from only one base class. *When to Use Both You can offer the best of both worlds, an interface and an abstract class. Implementors can ignore your abstract class if they choose. The only drawback of doing that is calling methods via their interface name is slightly slower than calling them via their abstract class name. Reference: http://mindprod.com/jgloss/interfacevsabstract.html

Question: 7 *One Answer Is Right*

Given:
```
class Plant {
   abstract String growthDirection();
}

class Embryophyta extends Plant {
   String growthDirection() { return "Up " }
}

public class Garden {
   public static void main(String[] args) {
      Embryophyta e = new Embryophyta();
      Embryophyta c = new Carrot();
      System.out.print(e.growthDirection() + growthDirection());
   }
}
```

What is the result?

Answers:

A) Up Down

B) Up Up

C) Up null

D) Compilation fails

E) An exception is thrown at runtime

Solution: D

Explanation:

Explanation: ------ Exception in thread "main" java.lang.ExceptionInInitializerError at garden.Garden.main Caused by: java.lang.RuntimeException: Uncompilable source code - garden.Plant is not abstract and does not override abstract method growthDirection() in garden.Plant

Question: 8 *One Answer Is Right*

Which four are syntactically correct?

Answers:

A) package abc; package def; import Java.util . * ; public class Test { }

B) package abc; import Java.util.*; import Java.util.regex.* ; public class Test { }

C) package abc; public class Test {} import Java.util.* ;

D) import Java.util.*; package abc; public class Test {}

E) package abc; import java.util. *; public class Test{}

F) public class Test{} package abc; import java.util.*{}

G) import java.util.*; public class Test{}

H) package abc; public class test {}

Solution: B, E, G, H

Question: 9 *One Answer Is Right*

Given:

```
interface Books {
    //insert code here
}
```

Which fragment, inserted in the Books interface, enables the code to compile?

Answers:

A) public abstract String type; public abstract String getType();

B) public static String type; public abstract String getType();

C) public String type = "Fiction"; public static String getType();

D) public String type = "Fiction"; public abstract String getType();

Solution: D

Question: 10 *One Answer Is Right*

Given:

```java
interface Event {
   String type = "Event";
   public void details();
}

class Quiz {
   static String type = "Quiz";
}

public class PracticeQuiz extends Quiz implements Event {
   public void details() {
      System.out.print(type);
   }

   public static void main(String[] args) {
      new PracticeQuiz().details();
      System.out.print(" " + type);
   }
}
```

What is the result?

Answers:

A) Event Quiz

B) Event Event

C) Quiz Quiz

D) Quiz Event

E) Compilation fails

Solution: E

Chapter 3: 1Z0-808 - Java SE 8 Programmer I

Exam Guide

Java 1Z0-808 Free Test is a test created to demonstrate all the features of our **Java8 Associate Web Simulator.** You will be able to access 25 complete questions and will have 53 minutes to finish the test.

There are several components you can interact with when you take our **mock exams:**

- Take a look at the progress bar at the top; it will tell how you are progressing throughout the exam.
- Read the question and select only the answer(s) you think are correct by checking the corresponding check box.
- Navigate the **Java Certification Questions** using the "Previous" and "Next" buttons.
- Mark the **Java Certification Questions** you wish to review later. All the questions you have marked will be listed in the right section "marked questions". You will be able to jump directly to the question from this list.
- if you want to take a look at the correct answers for a question, just click the **"Solution"** button. In the solution section you will be able to check your answers as well as find a full explanation.
- Keep an eye on the **countdown**. This will tell you how much time is left. When the countdown expires, the test

will be automatically submitted.

- Once the test is submitted, the **result** section will expand. Here, you will be able to review all the **questions of the test**. From here, you can also navigate directly to each question.

For more info visit: Oracle Java8 1Z0-808 Exam Reference

Oracle Java SE 8 Programmer I 1Z0-808 Exam:

Oracle Java SE 8 Programmer I 1Z0-808 Exam is related to the Oracle Java SE and Credits towards Oracle Certified Associate Java SE 8 Programmer and Oracle Certified Java Programmer Certification. This exam validates the ability to create executable Java Applications with a main method run a Java Program from the command line including console output determine the effect upon object references and primitive values when they are passed into methods that change the values develop code that demonstrates the use of polymorphisms including overriding and object type versus reference type differentiate among checked exceptions, unchecked exceptions, and errors. It also validates the ability to manipulate data using the string builder class and its methods and write a symbol lambda expression that consumes a lambda predicate expression application. Application Developers, Web Administrators, and Oracle Project Managers usually hold or pursue this certification and you can expect the same job role after completion of this certification.

1Z0-808 Exam topics:

Candidates must know the exam topics before they start of preparation. Because it will really help them in hitting the core. Our Oracle **1Z0-808 dumps** will include the following topics:

- Java Basics

- Using Operators and Decision Constructs
- Using Loop Constructs
- Working with Inheritance
- Working with Selected classes from the Java API
- Working With Java Data Types
- Creating and Using Arrays
- Working with Methods and Encapsulation
- Handling Exceptions

Certification Path:

There is no prerequisite for this exam.

Who should take the 1Z0-808 exam:

The Oracle Java SE 8 Programmer I 1Z0-808 Exam certification is an internationally-recognized validation that identifies persons who earn it as possessing skilled as an Oracle Certified Java Programmer. If a candidate wants significant improvement in career growth needs enhanced knowledge, skills, and talents. The Oracle Java SE 8 Programmer I 1Z0-808 Exam certification provides proof of this advanced knowledge and skill. If a candidate has knowledge of associated technologies and skills that are required to pass Oracle Java SE 8 Programmer I 1Z0-808 Exam then he should take this exam.

How to study the 1Z0-808 Exam:

There are two main types of resources for preparation of certification exams first there are the study guides and the books that are detailed and suitable for building knowledge from ground up then there are video tutorial and lectures that can somehow ease the pain of through study and are comparatively less boring for some candidates yet these demand time and concentration from the learner. Smart

Candidates who want to build a solid foundation in all exam topics and related technologies usually combine video lectures with study guides to reap the benefits of both but there is one crucial preparation tool as often overlooked by most candidates the practice exams. Practice exams are built to make students comfortable with the real exam environment. Statistics have shown that most students fail not due to that preparation but due to exam anxiety the fear of the unknown. Certification-questions.com expert team recommends you to prepare some notes on these topics along with it don't forget to practice Oracle **1Z0-808 dumps** which have been written by our expert team, Both these will help you a lot to clear this exam with good marks.

How much 1Z0-808 Exam Cost:

The price of the 1Z0-808 exam is $245 USD.

How to book the 1Z0-808 Exam:

These are following steps for registering the Oracle 1Z0-808 exam.
Step 1: Visit to Pearson Exam Registration
Step 2: Signup/Login to Pearson VUE account
Step 3: Search for Oracle 1Z0-808 Exam Certifications Exam
Step 4: Select Date, time and confirm with the payment method

What is the duration of the 1Z0-808 Exam:

- Format: Multiple choices, multiple answers
- Length of Examination: 150 minutes
- Number of Questions: 70
- Passing Score: 65%

The benefit in Obtaining the 1Z0-808 Exam Certification:

- Oracle Certified Java Programmer is distinguished among competitors. Oracle Certified Java Programmer certification can give them an edge at that time easily when candidates appear for a job interview employers seek to notify something which differentiates the individual to another.
- Oracle Certified Java Programmer have more useful and relevant networks that help them in setting career goals for themselves. Oracle Certified Java Programmer networks provide them with the right career direction than non certified usually are unable to get.
- Oracle Certified Java Programmer will be confident and stand different from others as their skills are more trained than non-certified professionals.
- Oracle Certified Java Programmer has the knowledge to use the tools to complete the task efficiently and cost-effectively than the other non-certified professionals lack in doing so.
- Oracle Certified Java Programmer Certification provides practical experience to candidates from all the aspects to be a proficient worker in the organization.
- Oracle Certified Java Programmer Certifications provide opportunities to get a job easily in which they are interested in instead of wasting years and ending without getting any experience.

Difficulty in writing 1Z0-808 Exam:

All Candidates wants to get success in the Oracle 1Z0-808 exam in the just first attempt but mostly not been able to get success in it due to poor selection of their Oracle 1Z0-808 training material. Certification-questions.com **Oracle 1Z0-808 dumps** are the perfect way to prepare Oracle 1Z0-808 exam to get good grades in the just first attempt. Certification-questions has quality Oracle 1Z0-808 pdf dumps and their Oracle Certified professionals designed them emphatically than others. Certification-questions is renowned across the globe just because of their quality study material So if candidates want instant success in the Oracle 1Z0-808 exam with quality Oracle 1Z0-808 training material then Certification-questions is the best option for you because our management is well trained in it and we update each question of all exams on regular basis after consulting recent updates with their Oracle certified professionals. It is very easy for the candidates to download **Oracle 1Z0-808 dumps** pdf from Certification-questions. With the help of **Oracle 1Z0-808 dumps**, candidates will get all the latest questions and answers for Oracle 1Z0-808 exam. We are confident that candidates can get a high score with excellent grades for the Oracle 1Z0-808 exam.

For more info visit::

Oracle 1Z0-808 Exam Reference

Sample Practice Test for 1Z0-808

Question: 1 *Multiple Answers Are Right*

Given the code fragment: public static void main(String[] args){ String date = LocalDate .parse("2014-05-04") .format(DateTimeFormatter.ISO_DATE_TIME) ; System.out.println(date); } What is the result?

Answers:

A) May 04, 2014T00:00:00.000

B) 2014-05-04T00:00: 00. 000

C) 5/4/14T00:00:00.000

D) An exception is thrown at runtime.

Solution: D

Explanation:

Explanation:java.time.temporal.UnsupportedTemporalTypeException: Unsupported field: HourOfDay

Question: 2 *Multiple Answers Are Right*

Given: class Mid { public int findMid(int n1, int n2) { return (n1 + n2) / 2; } } public class Calc extends Mid { public static void main(String[] args) { int n1 = 22, n2 = 2; //insert code here. System.out.print(n3); } } Which two code fragments, when inserted at // insert code here, enable the code to compile and print 12?

Answers:

A) Calc c = new Calc(); int n3 = c.findMid(n1,n2);

B) int n3 = super.findMid(n1,n3);

C) Calc c = new Mid(); int n3 = c.findMid(n1, n2);

D) Mid m1 = new Calc(); int n3 = m1.findMid(n1, n2);

E) int n3 = Calc.findMid(n1, n2);

Solution: A, D

Explanation:

Explanation: Incorrect: Not B: circular definition of n3. Not C: Compilation error. line Calc c = new Mid(); required: Calc found: Mid Not E: Compilation error. line int n3 = Calc.findMid(n1, n2); non-static method findMid(int,int) cannot be

Question: 3 *Multiple Answers Are Right*

Given: public class ComputeSum { int x; int y; public int sum; public ComputeSum (int nx, int ny) { x = nx; y =ny; updateSum(); } public void setX(int nx) { x = nx; updateSum();} public void setY(int ny) { x = ny; updateSum();} void updateSum() { sum = x + y;} } This class needs to protect an invariant on the sum field. Which three members must have the private access modifier to ensure that this invariant is maintained?

Answers:

A) The x field

B) The y field

C) The sum field

D) The ComputerSum ( ) constructor

E) The setX ( ) method

F) The setY ( ) method

Solution: C, E, F

Explanation:

Explanation:The sum field and the two methods (setX and SetY) that updates the sum field.

Question: 4 *Multiple Answers Are Right*

Which of the following can fill in the blank in this code to make it compile? (Select 2 options.) 1. public void method()____Exception { 2. _____Exception(); 3. }

Answers:

A) On line 1, fill in throws

B) On line 1, fill in throws new

C) On line 2, fill in throw new

D) On line 2, fill in throws

E) On line 2, fill in throws new

Solution: A, C

Explanation:

Explanation: Option A and C are the correct answer. In a method declaration, the keyword throws is used. So here at line 1 we have to use option A. To actually throw an exception, the keyword throw is used and a new exception is created, so at line 2 we have to use throw and new keywords, which is option C. Finally it will look like; public void method() throws Exception { throw new Exception0; } Reference : http://docs.oracle.com/javase/tutorial/essential/io/fileOps.html#

Question: 5 *Multiple Answers Are Right*

Which statement is true about the default constructor of a top-level class?

Answers:

A) It can take arguments.

B) It has private access modifier in its declaration.

C) It can be overloaded.

D) The default constructor of a subclass always invokes the no-argument constructor of its superclass.

Solution: D

Explanation:

Explanation: In both Java and C#, a "default constructor" refers to a nullary constructor that is automatically generated by the compiler if no constructors have been defined for the class. The default constructor is also empty, meaning that it does nothing. A programmer-defined constructor that takes no parameters is also called a default constructor.

Question: 6 *Multiple Answers Are Right*

Given: public class MyClass { public static void main(String[] args) { while (int ii = 0; ii < 2) { ii++; System.out.println("ii = " + ii); } } } What is the result?

Answers:

A) ii = 1 ii = 2

B) Compilation fails

C) The program prints nothing

D) The program goes into an infinite loop with no output

E) The program goes to an infinite loop outputting: ii = 1 ii = 1

Solution: B

Explanation:

Explanation: The while statement is incorrect. It has the syntax of a for statement. The while statement continually executes a block of statements while a particular condition is true. Its syntax can be expressed as: while (expression) { statement(s) } The while statement evaluates expression, which must return a boolean value. If the expression evaluates to true, the while statement executes the statement(s) in the while block. The while statement continues testing the expression and executing its block until the expression evaluates to false. Reference: The while and do-while Statements

Question: 7 *Multiple Answers Are Right*

Given: public class MarkList { int num; public static void graceMarks(MarkList obj4) { obj4.num += 10; } public static void main(String[] args) { MarkList obj1 = new MarkList(); MarkList obj2 = obj1; MarkList obj3 = new MarkList(); obj2.num = 60; graceMarks(obj2); } } How many objects are created in the memory runtime?

Answers:

A) 1

B) 2

C) 3

D) 4

Solution: B

Explanation:

Explanation: obj1 and obj3. when you do obj2 = obj1 you're copying object references - you're not making a copy of the object - and so the variables obj1 and obj2 will both point to the same object.

Question: 8 *Multiple Answers Are Right*

Given the classes: * AssertionError * ArithmeticException * ArrayIndexOutOfBoundsException * FileNotFoundException * IllegalArgumentException * IOError * IOException * NumberFormatException * SQLException Which option lists only those classes that belong to the unchecked exception category?

Answers:

A) ArrayIndexOutOfBoundsException, ArithmeticException

B) AssertionError, IOError, IOException

C) ArithmeticException, FileNotFoundException, NumberFormatException

D) FileNotFoundException, IOException, SQLException

E) ArrayIndexOutOfBoundException, IllegalArgumentException, FileNotFoundException

Solution: A

Explanation:

Explanation: Not B: IOError and IOException are both checked errors. Not C, not D, not E: FileNotFoundException is a checked error. Note: Checked exceptions: * represent invalid conditions in areas outside the immediate control of the program (invalid user input, database problems, network outages, absent files) * are subclasses of Exception * a method is obliged to establish a policy for all checked exceptions thrown by its implementation (either pass the checked exception further up the stack, or handle it somehow) Note: Unchecked exceptions: * represent defects in the program (bugs) - often invalid arguments passed to a non-private method. To quote from The Java Programming

Language, by Gosling, Arnold, and Holmes: "Unchecked runtime exceptions represent conditions that, generally speaking, reflect errors in your program's logic and cannot be reasonably recovered from at run time." * are subclasses of RuntimeException, and are usually implemented using IllegalArgumentException, NullPointerException, or IllegalStateException * method is not obliged to establish a policy for the unchecked exceptions thrown by its implementation (and they almost always do not do so)

Question: 9 *Multiple Answers Are Right*

Given: abstract class X { public abstract void methodX(); } interface Y{ public void methodY(); } Which two code fragments are valid? A) class Z extends X implements Y { public void methodZ(){} } B) abstract class Z extends X implements Y { public void methodZ(){} } C) class Z extends X implements Y { public void methodX(){} public void methodY(){} } D) abstract class Z extends X implements Y { } E) class Z extends X implements Y { public void methodY(){} }

Answers:

A) Option A

B) Option B

C) Option C

D) Option D

E) Option E

Solution: B, C, D

Explanation:

Explanation: When an abstract class is subclassed, the subclass usually provides implementations for all of the abstract methods in its parent class (C). However, if it does not, then the subclass must also be declared abstract (B)(D). Note: An abstract class is a class that is declared abstract--it may or may not include abstract methods. Abstract classes cannot be instantiated, but they can be subclassed.

Question: 10 *Multiple Answers Are Right*

Which of the following data types will allow the following code snippet to compile? float i=4; float j=2; ___z=i+j;

Answers:

A) long

B) double

C) int

D) float

E) byte

Solution: B, D

Explanation:

Explanation: Option B and D are the correct answer. Since the variables i and j are floats, resultant will be float type too. So we have to use float or primitive type which can hold float, such a primitive type is double, it has wider range and also can hold floating point numbers, hence we can use double or float for the blank. As explained above options B and D are correct. long and int can't be used with floating point numbers so option A is incorrect. Option E is incorrect as it have smaller range and also can't be used with floating point numbers.

Reference:http://docs.oracle.com/javase/tutorial/java/javaOO/variables.html

Chapter 4: 1Z0-809 - Java SE 8 Programmer II

Exam Guide

Oracle Java SE 8 Programmer II 1Z0-809 Exam:

Oracle Java SE 8 Programmer II 1Z0-809 Exam is related to Oracle Java SE and credits toward Oracle Certified Professional and Java SE 8 Programmer Certification. This exam is part second of the Java SE 8 Programmer. This exam validates the ability to develop code that uses the static keyword on blocks, variables, methods and chases, implements and intends interfaces and use the at override annotation, search for data by using search methods of the stream classes, save results to a collection. It also validates the ability to create and manage date-based and time-based events including a combination of date and time int a single object. Java EE Developers, Web Developers and Java Developers usually hold or pursue this certification and you can expect the same job role after completion of this certification.

1Z0-809 Exam topics:

Candidates must know the exam topics before they start of preparation. Because it will really help them in hitting the core. Our Oracle **1Z0-809 dumps** will include the following topics:

- Java Class Design
- Generics and Collections

- Java Stream API
- Use Java SE 8 Date/Time API
- Java File I/O (NIO.2)
- Building Database Applications with JDBC
- Advanced Java Class Design
- Lambda Built-in Functional Interfaces
- Exceptions and Assertions
- Java I/O Fundamentals
- Java Concurrency
- Localization

Certification Path:

Oracle Java SE 8 Programmer I can act as a prerequisite for this 1Z0-809 exam.

Who should take the 1Z0-809 exam:

The Oracle Java SE 8 Programmer II 1Z0-809 Exam certification is an internationally-recognized validation that identifies persons who earn it as possessing skilled as an Oracle Certified Java Programmer. If a candidate wants significant improvement in career growth needs enhanced knowledge, skills, and talents. The Oracle Java SE 8 Programmer II 1Z0-809 Exam certification provides proof of this advanced knowledge and skill. If a candidate has knowledge of associated technologies and skills that are required to pass Oracle Java SE 8 Programmer II 1Z0-809 Exam then he should take this exam.

How to study the 1Z0-809 Exam:

There are two main types of resources for preparation of certification exams first there are the study guides and the books that are detailed and suitable for building knowledge from ground up then there are video tutorial and lectures that can somehow ease the pain of through study and are comparatively less boring for some candidates yet these demand time and concentration from the learner. Smart Candidates who want to build a solid foundation in all exam topics and related technologies usually combine video lectures with study guides to reap the benefits of both but there is one crucial preparation tool as often overlooked by most candidates the practice exams. Practice exams are built to make students comfortable with the real exam environment. Statistics have shown that most students fail not due to that preparation but due to exam anxiety the fear of the unknown. Certification-questions.com expert team recommends you to prepare some notes on these topics along with it don't forget to practice Oracle **1Z0-809 dumps** which have been written by our expert team, Both these will help you a lot to clear this exam with good marks.

How much 1Z0-809 Exam Cost:

The price of the 1Z0-809 exam is $245 USD.

How to book the 1Z0-809 Exam:

These are following steps for registering the Oracle 1Z0-809 exam.
Step 1: Visit to Pearson Exam Registration
Step 2: Signup/Login to Pearson VUE account
Step 3: Search for Oracle 1Z0-809 Exam Certifications Exam
Step 4: Select Date, time and confirm with the payment method

What is the duration of the 1Z0-809 Exam:

- Format: Multiple choices, multiple answers
- Length of Examination: 150 minutes
- Number of Questions: 85
- Passing Score: 65%

The benefit in Obtaining the 1Z0-809 Exam Certification:

- Oracle Certified Java Programmer is distinguished among competitors. Oracle Certified Java Programmer certification can give them an edge at that time easily when candidates appear for a job interview employers seek to notify something which differentiates the individual to another.
- Oracle Certified Java Programmer have more useful and relevant networks that help them in setting career goals for themselves. Oracle Certified Java Programmer networks provide them with the right career direction than non certified usually are unable to get.
- Oracle Certified Java Programmer will be confident and stand different from others as their skills are more trained than non-certified professionals.
- Oracle Certified Java Programmer has the knowledge to use the tools to complete the task efficiently and cost-effectively than the other non-certified professionals lack in doing so.
- Oracle Certified Java Programmer Certification provides practical experience to candidates from all the aspects to be a proficient worker in the organization.
- Oracle Certified Java Programmer Certifications provide opportunities to get a job easily in which they are interested in instead of wasting years and ending without getting any experience.

Difficulty in writing 1Z0-809 Exam:

Oracle Certified Java Programmer is the most powerful certification that candidates can have on their resume. But for this, they will have to pass Oracle 1Z0-809 questions. Oracle 1Z0-809 is a challenging exam to pass this exam Candidates will have to work hard with the help of right focus and preparation material passing this exam is an achievable goal. Certification-questions help candidates by providing the most relevant and updated **Oracle 1Z0-809 dumps**. Furthermore, We also provide the Oracle 1Z0-809 practice test that will be much beneficial in the preparation. Certification-questions aims to provide the best **Oracle 1Z0-809 dumps** that is verified by the Oracle experts. If Candidates feel any doubt in the Oracle 1Z0-809 practice test then our team is always there to help them. **Oracle 1Z0-809 dumps** are the perfect way to prepare Oracle 1Z0-809 exam with good grades in the just first attempt. So, Candidates want instant success in the Oracle 1Z0-809 exam with quality Oracle 1Z0-809 training material then Certification-questions is the best option for them because our management is well trained in it and we update each question of all exams on regular basis after consulting recent updates with our Oracle certified professionals.

For more info visit::

Oracle 1Z0-809 Exam Reference

Java 1Z0-809 Free Test is a test created to demonstrate all the features of our **Java8 Professional Web Simulator.** You will be able to access 25 full questions and will have 44 minutes to finish the test.

There are several components you can interact with when you take our **mock exams:**

- Take a look at the progress bar at the top; it will tell how you are progressing throughout the exam.
- Read the question and select only the answer(s) you think are correct by checking the corresponding check box.
- Navigate the **Java Certification Questions** using the "Previous" and "Next" buttons.

- Mark the **Java Certification Questions** you wish to review later. All the questions you have marked will be listed in the right section "marked questions". You will be able to jump directly to the question from this list.
- if you want to take a look at the correct answers for a question, just click the **"Solution"** button. In the solution section you will be able to check your answers as well as find a full explanation.
- Keep an eye on the **countdown**. This will tell you how much time is left. When the countdown expires, the test will be automatically submitted.
- Once the test is submitted, the **result** section will expand. Here, you will be able to review all the **questions of the test**. From here, you can also navigate directly to each question.

For more info visit: Oracle Java8 1Z0-809 Exam Reference

Sample Practice Test for 1Z0-809

Question: 1 *One Answer Is Right*

Consider the following class: public final class Program { final private String name; Program (String name){ this.name = name; getName(); } //code here } Which of the following codes will make an instance of this class immutable?

Answers:

A) public String getName(){return name;}

B) public String getName(String value){ name=value; return value;}

C) private String getName(){return name+"a";}

D) public final String getName(){return name+="a";}

E) All of Above.

Solution: A, C

Explanation:

Option B and D have a compile error since name variable is final. Option C is private and doesn't change the name value. Option A is public and doesn't change the name value. Exam Objective : Encapsulation and Subclassing - Making classes immutable. Oracle Reference : https://docs.oracle.com/javase/tutorial/essential/concurrency/imstrat.html

Question: 2 *One Answer Is Right*

Given the following class: 1. public class Test { 2. public static void main(String args[]) { 3. //Code Here 4. Thread thread = new Thread(r); 5. thread.start(); 6. } 7. } Which of the following lines will give a valid Thread creation?

Answers:

A) Thread r = () -> System.out.println("Running");

B) Run r = () -> System.out.println("Running");

C) Runnable r = () -> System.out.println("Running");

D) Executable r = () -> System.out.println("Running");

E) None Of Above

Solution: C

Explanation:

Option A,B, and D are incorrect as they are not functional interfaces, so C is the only valid option. Exam Objective : Concurrency - Creating worker threads using Runnable and Callable. Oracle Reference : https://docs.oracle.com/javase/tutorial/essential/concurrency/

Question: 3 *One Answer Is Right*

Given the following class: 1. class Singleton { 2. private int count = 0; 3. private Singleton(){}; 4. public static final Singleton getInstance(){ return new Singleton(); }; 5. public void add(int i){ count+=i; }; 6. public int getCount(){ return count;}; 7. } 8. 9. public class Program { 10. public static void main(String[] args) { 11. Singleton s1 = Singleton.getInstance(); 12. s1.add(3); 13. Singleton s2 = Singleton.getInstance(); 14. s2.add(2); 15. Singleton s3 = Singleton.getInstance(); 16. s2.add(1); 17. System.out.println(s1.getCount()+s2.getCount()+s3.getCount()); 18. } 19. } What will be the result?

Answers:

A) 18

B) 7

C) 6

D) The code will not compile.

E) None of above

Solution: C

Explanation:

The class "Singleton" is not a real singleton class, in fact at each "getInstance()" method invocation a new object is created, so s1, s2, s3 count instance variable are 3, 2, 1, and then option C is correct. Exam Objective : Java Class Design - Create and use singleton classes and immutable classes Oracle Reference : https://docs.oracle.com/javase/tutorial/essential/concurrency/imstrat.html

Question: 4 *One Answer Is Right*

Given the following class: 1. public class Program { 2. 3. public static void main(String[] args) { 4. 5. List list = Arrays.asList(4,6,12,66,3); 6. 7. String s = list.stream().map(i -> { 8. return ""+(i+1); 9. }).reduce("", String::concat); 10. 11. System.out.println(s); 12. } 13. } What will be the result?

Answers:

A) 4612663

B) 5713674

C) 3661264

D) The code will not compile because of line 7.

E) Unhandled exception type NumberFormatException al line 8.

Solution: B

Explanation:

The Program is applying a map function to the stream generated from list. For each Integer element "i" the function returns a new String with value i+1. The stream is then reduced to a String by the concatenation "String::concat" function. So Option B is correct, and A ,C, D, E are incorrect. Exam Objective :

Collections Streams, and Filters - Iterating through a collection using lambda syntax Oracle Reference : https://docs.oracle.com/javase/8/docs/api/java/util/stream/package-summary.html

Question: 5 *One Answer Is Right*

Consider the following class: 1. public class Test { 2. public static int count(T[] array, T elem) { 3. int count = 0; 4. for (T e : array) 5. if(e.compareTo(elem) > 0) ++count; 6. 7. return count; 8. } 9. public static void main(String[] args) { 10. Integer[] a = {1,2,3,4,5}; 11. int n = Test.count(a, 3); 12. System.out.println(n); 13. } 14. } What will be the result?

Answers:

A) 2

B) 3

C) The code will not compile because of line 5.

D) An exception is thrown.

E) None of Above.

Solution: C

Explanation:

C is correct because the variable "e" is a generic "T" type so the compile has no knowledge of method "compareTo". In order to make it compile line 2 needs to be changed in: public static > int count(T[] array, T elem) { Exam Objective : Collections and Generics - Creating a custom generic class Oracle Reference : https://docs.oracle.com/javase/tutorial/java/generics/methods.html

Question: 6 *One Answer Is Right*

Given the following class: 1. public class Program { 2. public static void main(String[] args) { 3. 4. Thread th = new Thread(new Runnable(){ 5. 6. static { 7. System.out.println("initial"); 8. } 9. 10. @Override 11. public void run() { 12. System.out.println("start"); 13. } 14. }); 15. 16. th.start(); 17. } 18. } What will be the result?

Answers:

A) start initial

B) initial start

C) initial

D) A runtime exception is thrown.

E) The code will not compile because of line 6.

Solution: E

Explanation:

Because you cannot declare static initializers in an anonymous class, the compilation fails at line 6, so E is correct and A, B, C, D are incorrect. Exam Objective : Interfaces and Lambda Expressions - Anonymous inner classes Oracle Reference : https://docs.oracle.com/javase/tutorial/java/javaOO/anonymousclasses.html

Question: 7 *One Answer Is Right*

Consider the following class: 1. final class A{ 2. private String s; 3. public A(String s){ 4. this.s = s; 5. } 6. public String toString(){ return s; }; 7. public void setA(String a){ this.s+= a; }; 8. } 9. 10. public final class Immutable { 11. private final A a; 12. public Immutable(A a){ 13. this.a = a; 14. } 15. public String toString(){ return a.toString();}; 16. public static void main(String[] args){

17. 18. A a = new A("Bye"); 19. Immutable im = new Immutable(a); 20. System.out.print(im); 21. 22. a.setA(" bye"); 23. System.out.print(im); 24. } 25. } What will be the result?

Answers:

A) Bye bye

B) Bye Bye

C) ByeBye bye

D) Compilation failure

E) None of Above

Solution: C

Explanation:

In order for the class "immutable" to be an immutable class it needs to satisfy the following four properties: 1.Don't provide "setter" methods - methods that modify fields or objects reffered to by fields. 2. Make all fields final and private. 3. Don't allow subclasses to override methods. The simplest way to do this is to declare the class as final. A more sophisticated approach is to make the constructor private and construct instances in factory methods. 4. If the instance fields include references to mutable objects, don't allow those objects to be changed. Properties 1,2,3 are satisfied, but unfortunately the last one is not, so the object "a" is mutable because it is passed by reference without making a protection copy of it. So option C is correct and A,B,D,E are incorrect. Exam Objective : Encapsulation and Subclassing - Making classes immutable. Oracle Reference : https://docs.oracle.com/javase/tutorial/essential/concurrency/imstrat.html

Question: 8 *One Answer Is Right*

Given the following code: 1. // Code Here 2. @Override 3. public void run() { 4. for(int i = 0;i<10;i++) 5. System.out.print(i); 6. } 7. } 8. 9. public class Test { 10. public static void main(String args[]) { 11. Task t = new Task(); 12. Thread thread = new Thread(t); 13. thread.start(); 14. } 15. } Which of the following lines will give the result 0123456789?

Answers:

A) class Task extends Runnable {

B) class Task implements Runnable {

C) class Task implements Thread {

D) class Task extends Thread {

E) None Of Above

Solution: B

Explanation:

We can create a Thread by passing an implementation of Runnable to a Thread constructor, so the only correct option is B. Exam Objective : Concurrency - Creating worker threads using Runnable and Callable. Oracle Reference : https://docs.oracle.com/javase/tutorial/essential/concurrency/

Question: 9 *One Answer Is Right*

Consider the following class: 1. public class Program { 2. 3. public static void main(String[] args){ 4. 5. Callable c = new Callable(){ 6. @Override 7. public String call() throws Exception { 8. String s=""; 9. for (int i = 0; i < 10; i++) { s+=i;} 10. return s; 11. } 12. }; 13. 14. ExecutorService executor =

Executors.newSingleThreadExecutor(); 15. Future future = executor.submit(c); 16. try { 17. String result = future.wait(); 18. System.out.println(result); 19. } catch (ExecutionException e) { 20. e.printStackTrace(); 21. } 22. } 23. } What will be the result?

Answers:

A) 0123456789

B) 12345678910

C) Unhandled exception type InterruptedException al line 17

D) The code will not compile because of line 5.

E) The code will not compile because of line 17.

Solution: E

Explanation:

We are creating a Callable object with an anonymous class at line 5, the syntax is correct so option C is incorrect. Passing the object "c" to an executor will get as return type a Future to wait for thread ends. But at line 17 method wait of Class Future doesn't exist so E is correct. Exam Objective : Concurrency - Creating worker threads using Runnable and Callable. Oracle Reference : https://docs.oracle.com/javase/tutorial/essential/concurrency/

Question: 10 *One Answer Is Right*

Which of the following are valid Executors factory methods? I. ExecutorService es1 = Executors.newSingleThreadExecutor(4); II. ExecutorService es1 = Executors.newFixedThreadPool(10); III. ExecutorService es1 = Executors.newScheduledThreadPool(); IV. ExecutorService es1

= Executors.newScheduledThreadPool(10); V. ExecutorService es1 = Executors.newSingleThreadScheduledExecutor();

Answers:

A) I, II, III

B) II, III, IV, V

C) I, IV, V

D) II, IV, V

E) All

Solution: D

Explanation:

The method "newSingleThreadExecutor" cannot accept parameters so I is incorrect, and the method "newScheduledThreadPool" with parameters doesn't exist so III is incorrect. Exam Objective : Concurrency - Using an ExecutorService to concurrently execute tasks. Oracle Reference :

https://docs.oracle.com/javase/tutorial/essential/concurrency/

Chapter 5: 1Z0-813 - Upgrade to Java SE 8 OCP

Exam Guide

1z0-813 - Upgrade to Java SE 8 OCP:

1z0-813 exam is part of the new Oracle Certified Professional - Java SE 8 Programmer certification. This exam measures your ability and skills related to Java SE 8 Programming include Language Enhancements, Concurrency, Localization, Java File I/O, Lambda, Java Collections, and Java Streams.

Our 1z0-813 dumps will include those topics::

- Enhancements
- Concurrency
- Localization
- Java File I/O
- Lambda
- Java Collections
- Java Streams.

For more info visit: 1z0-813 Exam Reference

Certification Path:

The Oracle Certified Professional - Java SE 8 Programmer certification requires the following certification before taking 1z0-813 exam.

- Java SE 6 any previous versions

Who should take the exam:

if you have the following prerequisite and required skills then you should take this exam for getting Oracle Certified Professional - Java SE 8 Programmer certificate.

- Have experience and skills of Java 6 or previous version programming
- Have expertise in Java 8 programming

How to study 1z0-813 Exam:

Oracle offered the following courses to help you prepare for the certification tests.

- Java SE 7 new features
- Java SE 8 new features

This course is recommended, but not required, before taking a 1z0-813 certification exam. When preparing for the 1z0-813 certification exam, keep in mind that real world experience is required to stand a reasonable chance of passing 1z0-813 exam.

How much 1z0-813 Exam Cost:

The price of the exam is 245 USD.

How to book 1z0-813 Exam:

Register for Oracle Certified Professional - Java SE 8 Programmer Certification Exam on Pearson VUE

What is the duration of 1z0-813 Exam:

The duration of this exam is 130 minutes

Benefit in Obtaining the Exam Certification:

- Certified Oracle Certified Professional - Java SE 8 Programmer report high job satisfaction
- Company decision makers see value in certification

Exam Difficulty:

When preparing for the 1z0-813 certification exam, the real world experience is required to stand a reasonable chance of passing 1z0-813 exam. Oracle recommended courses does not replace the requirement for experience. So, It is very difficult for the candidate to pass the 1z0-813 exam without experience.

Why use Certification-questions.com to study:

Certification-questions.com is a central hub for all people looking for information and resources regarding certification exams we create an extremely accurate and loyal web and mobile exam simulator. Certification-questions is providing a set of 1z0-813 exam questions with the answers. 1z0-813 practice exams have been built to imitate the real exam.

Which candidate knowledge the exam will verify:

The 1z0-813 certification exam will verify that the successful candidate has important knowledge and skills necessary to Java SE 8 Programming include Language Enhancements, Concurrency, Localization, Java File I/O, Lambda, Java Collections, and Java Streams.

Advantage in the Career after to pass the Certification Exam:

Having an Oracle Certified Professional - Java SE 8 Programmer certification will certainly give you an advantage when hiring managers to look at your resume. If you have certification is a significant advantage in jobs competition as compared to those who do not have one. If you have the certificate then you can move up the corporate ladder or into a better, higher-paying job in your company. You can also join a unique group of certified and skilled professionals. There are many companies that support their employees in earning these certifications that may even lead to promotions and raises as well. Many companies have requirements by their professional recertify every two to three years.

Market Trends:

The Oracle Certified Professional - Java SE 8 Programmer Certification exam contains a high value in the market is the brand value of the Oracle attached with it.

Sample Practice Test for 1Z0-813

Question: 1 *One Answer Is Right*

Which two statements are true about localizing an application? (Choose two.)

Answers:

A) Language codes use lowercase and region codes use uppercase letters.

B) Resource bundle files include date and currency information.

C) Language and region-specific programs are created using localized data.

D) Support for new regional languages does not require recompilation of the code.

E) Textual elements (messages and GUI labels) are hard-coded on the code.

Solution: A, C

Explanation:

Explanation: A: The following examples create Locale objects for the French language in Canada, the English language in the U.S. and Great Britain. aLocale = new Locale("fr", "CA"); bLocale = new Locale("en", "US"); cLocale = new Locale("en", "GB"); C: Localization is the process of adapting an internationalized application to support a specific region or locale. Incorrect Answers: B: Resource bundle files does not include date a currency information. Date and currency information are stored in locales, not in resource bundle files. D: Recompilation is not necessary. E: Textual elements are not hard-coded on the code. References: https://docs.oracle.com/javase/tutorial/i18n/locale/create.html http://docs.oracle.com/javaee/6/tutorial/doc/bnaxw.html

Question: 2 *One Answer Is Right*

Given:

```
class Washer {
    public static void main (String[] args) {
        Runnable r = () -> {
            System.out.print("L1 ");
        };
        new Thread(r) .start();
        new Thread(() -> {
            System.out.print("L2 ");
        }) .start();
        System.out.print("L3 ");
    }
}
```

Which result is possible?

Answers:

A) Compilation fails.

B) L1 L2 L3

C) L2 L3

D) L1 L3

E) L3

Solution: B

Explanation:

Explanation: The Runnable interface should be implemented by any class whose instances are intended to be executed by a thread. The class must define a method of no arguments called run. This interface is designed to provide a common protocol for objects that wish to execute code while they are active.
Reference:
http://docs.oracle.com/javase/7/docs/api/java/lang/Runnable.html

Question: 3 *One Answer Is Right*

Given the fragment:

```
public static void main(String[] args) {
    List<String> sList = Arrays.asList("A", "B", "C", "D");
    //line n1
    System.out.println(str);
}
```

Which code fragment, when inserted at line n1, enables the code to print ABCD?

Answers:

A) String str = sList.stream().reduce("",(s1, s2) -> s1.concat(s2));

B) String str = sList.stream().reduce("A",(s1, s2) -> s1.concat(s2));

C) String str = sList.stream().reduce((s1, s2) -> s1.concat(s2));

D) String str = sList.stream().reduce("A",String::concat);

Solution: A

Explanation:

Explanation: The java.util.Arrays.asList(T... a) returns a fixed-size list backed by the specified array. Note: Use the following import statements to be able to run the code. import java.util.Arrays; import java.util.List; Incorrect Answers: B, D: Output is AABCD Reference: https://www.tutorialspoint.com/java/util/arrays_aslist.htm

Question: 4 *One Answer Is Right*

Given the code fragment:

```
final List<String> list = new CopyOnWriteArrayList<>();
final AtomicInteger ai = new AtomicInteger(0);
final CyclicBarrier narrier = new CyclicBarrier(2, new Runnable() {
    public void run() {System.out.println(list); }
});
Runnable r = new Runnable() {
    public void run() {
        try {
            Thread.sleep(1000 * ai.incrementAndGet());
        } catch (Exception ex) {
        }
    }
};
new Thread(r).start();
new Thread(r).start();
new Thread(r).start();
new Thread(r).start();
```

What is the result?

Answers:

A) [x, x] [x, x, x, x]

B) [x, x]

C) [x] [x, x] [x, x, x]

D) [x] [x, x] [x, x, x] [x, x, x, x]

Solution: D

Explanation:

Explanation: CyclicBarrier is a synchronization aid that allows a set of threads to all wait for each other to reach a common barrier point. CyclicBarriers are useful in programs involving a fixed sized party of threads that must occasionally wait for each other. The barrier is called cyclic because it can be re-used after the waiting threads are released. Reference: https://docs.oracle.com/javase/7/docs/api/java/util/concurrent/CyclicBarrier.html

Question: 5 *One Answer Is Right*

Given:

```
class Person {
    private String firstName;
    private int salsary;
    public Person(String fN, int sal) {
        this.firstName = fN;
        this.salary = sal;
    }
    public int getSalary() { return salary; }
    public String getFirstName() {return firstName; }
}
```

and the code fragment:

```
List<Person> prog = Arrays.asList(
        new Person("Smith", 1500),
        new Person("John", 2000),
        new Person("Joe", 1000));
double dVal = prog.stream()
        .filter(s -> s.getFirstName().startsWith("J"))
        .mapToInt(Person::getSalary)
        .average()
        .getAsDouble();
System.out.print(dVal);
```

What is the result?

Answers:

A) A compilation error occurs.

B) 2000.0

C) 1500.0

D) 0.0

Solution: A

Explanation:

Explanation: The line mapToInt(Person::GetSalary) will cause a compile error. If it is replaced by the following line, a "." is added in the beginning of the line, the result would be 1500.0: .mapToInt(Person::getSalary)

Question: 6 *One Answer Is Right*

Given the code fragment:

```
//line n1
Double d = str.average().getAsDouble();
System.out.println("Average = " + d);
```

Which should be inserted into the line n1 to print Average = 2.5?

Answers:

A) Stream str = Stream.of(1, 2, 3, 4);

B) IntStream str = IntStream.of(1, 2, 3, 4);

C) DoubleStream str = Stream.of(1.0, 2.0, 3.0, 4.0);

D) IntStream str = Stream.of(1, 2, 3, 4)

Solution: B

Explanation:

Explanation: Use IntStream. Reference: https://docs.oracle.com/javase/8/docs/api/java/util/stream/IntStream.html

Question: 7 *One Answer Is Right*

Given the code fragment:

```
public class TestString {
    public static void main(String[] args) {
        String str=null;

        switch(str) {
            case "":
                System.out.println("blank"); break;
            case "null":
                System.out.println("NULL"); break;
            default:
                System.out.println("invalid");
        }
    }
}
```

What is the result?

Answers:

A) invalid

B) An exception is thrown at runtime.

C) NULL

D) Compilation fails.

E) blank

Solution: B

Explanation:

Explanation: A java.lang.NullPointerException is through at line switch(str) {.

Question: 8 *One Answer Is Right*

In 2015. daylight saving time in New York, USA, begins on March 8th at 2:00 AM. As a result, 2:00 AM becomes 3:00 AM. Given the code fragment:

```
ZoneId zone = ZoneId.of("America/New_York");
ZonedDateTime dt = ZonedDateTime.of(LocalDate.of(2015, 3, 8), LocalTime.of(1, 0), zone);
ZonedDateTime dt2 = dt.plusHours(2);
System.out.print(DateTimeFormatter.ofPattern("H:mm - ").format(dt2));
System.out.println("difference: " + ChronoUnit.HOURS.between(dt, dt2));
```

Which is the result?

Answers:

A) 2:00 – difference: 1

B) 3:00 – difference: 2

C) 4:00 – difference: 3

D) 4:00 – difference: 2

Solution: D

Explanation:

Explanation: Reference:
http://docs.oracle.com/javase/8/docs/api/java/time/ZoneId.html

Question: 9 *One Answer Is Right*

Given the code fragment:

```
List<StringBuilder> names = new ArrayList<>();
names.add(new StringBuilder("Tom"));
names.add(new StringBuilder("Joe"));
names.stream().forEach(s -> s.append("Hello"));
names.forEach(s -> {
    s.insert(3, ",");
    System.out.println(s);
});
```

What is the result?

Answers:

A) A compilation error occurs.

B) An IllegalStateException is thrown at run time.

C) Tom, Hello Joe, Hello

D) Tom, Joe,

Solution: C

Explanation:

Explanation: Output: Tom,Hello Joe,Hello

Question: 10 *One Answer Is Right*

Given the code fragment:

```java
List<String> qwords = Arrays.asList("why ", "what ", "when ");
BinaryOperator<String> operator = (s1, s2) -> s1.concat(s2);
String sen = qwords.stream()
    .reduce("Word: ", operator);
System.out.println(sen);
```

What is the result?

Answers:

A) Word: why what when

B) Words: why Word: Why what Word: why what when

C) Word: why Word: what Word: when

D) Compilation fails.

Solution: A

Chapter 6: 1Z0-815 - Java SE 11 Programmer I

Exam Guide

How to Prepare For 1Z0-815:Java SE 11 Programmer Exam

Preparation Guide for 1Z0-815:Java SE 11 Programmer Exam

Introduction

Java has introduced certification path for all the participants who looking to get certified in server administration on the windows platform. This certification program provides Java server administration professionals a way to demonstrate their skills. The assessment is based on a rigorous exam using industry standard methodology to determine whether a candidate meets Java's proficiency standards.

According to Java, a Java Certified Professional enables organizations to leverage Java windows server management, Java 1Z0-815:Java SE 11 Programmer Exam is designed for professional who are working in the IT industries as well as it focuses on the other candidates who want to prove introductory knowledge of Windows Server.

Certification is evidence of your skills, expertise in those areas in which you like to work. There are many vendors in the market that are providing these certifications. If candidate wants to work on 1Z0-815:Java SE 11 Programmer Exam and prove his knowledge, Certification offered by Java. This **1Z0-815 Java Exam** helps a candidate to validates his skills in 1Z0-815:Java SE 11 Programmer Exam Technology.

In this guide, we will cover the 1Z0-815:Java SE 11 Programmer Exam Certification, 1Z0-815:Java SE 11 Programmer Exam Certified professional salary and all aspects of the 1Z0-815:Java SE 11 Programmer Exam Certification.

Introduction to 1Z0-815:Java SE 11 Programmer Exam:

1Z0-815 Java Exam is a certification exam that is conducted by Java to validates candidate knowledge and skills of Managing Projects and Portfolios.

Java SE 11 Developer certification comes with eminent significance in this technology world. Owing to its rigorous and extensive coverage of the essentially advanced concepts of Java (Standard Edition) 11, possessor of this certification is deemed as the ideal professional for Java-based programming and application development.

After passing this exam, candidates get a certificate from Java that helps them to demonstrate their proficiency in Windows Server Fundamentals to their clients and employers.

Topics of 1Z0-815:Java SE 11 Programmer Exam:

Candidates must know the exam topics before they start of preparation. because it will really help them in hitting the core. Our **1Z0-815 Java dumps** will include the following topics:

1. Understanding Java Technology and environment

- Describe Java Technology and the Java development
- Identify key features of the Java language

2. Working With Java Primitive Data Types and String APIs

- Declare and initialize variables (including casting and promoting primitive data types)
- Identify the scope of variables
- Use local variable type inference
- Create and manipulate Strings
- Manipulate data using the StringBuilder class and its methods

3. Working with Java Arrays

- Declare, instantiate, initialize and use a one-dimensional array
- Declare, instantiate, initialize and use a two-dimensional array

4. Creating and Using Methods

- Create methods and constructors with arguments and return values
- Create and invoke overloaded methods
- Apply the static keyword to methods and fields

5. Reusing Implementations Through Inheritance

- Create and use subclasses and superclasses
- Create and extend abstract classes
- Enable polymorphism by overriding methods
- Utilize polymorphism to cast and call methods, differentiating object type versus reference type
- Distinguish overloading, overriding, and hiding

6. Handling Exceptions

- Describe the advantages of Exception handling and differentiate among checked, unchecked exceptions, and Errors
- Create try-catch blocks and determine how exceptions alter program flow
- Create and invoke a method that throws an exception

7. Creating a Simple Java Program

- Create an executable Java program with a main class
- Compile and run a Java program from the command line
- Create and import packages

8. Using Operators and Decision Constructs

- Use Java operators including the use of parentheses to override operator precedence
- Use Java control statements including if, if/else, switch
- Create and use do/while, while, for and for each loops, including nested loops, use break and continue statements

9. Describing and Using Objects and Classes

- Declare and instantiate Java objects, and explain objects' lifecycles (including creation, dereferencing by reassignment, and garbage collection)
- Define the structure of a Java class
- Read or write to object fields

10. Applying Encapsulation

- Apply access modifiers
- Apply encapsulation principles to a class

11. Programming Abstractly Through Interfaces

- Create and implement interfaces

- Distinguish class inheritance from interface inheritance including abstract classes
- Declare and use List and ArrayList instances
- Understanding Lambda Expressions

12. Understanding Modules

- Describe the Modular JDK
- Declare modules and enable access between modules
- Describe how a modular project is compiled and run

Who should take the 1Z0-815:Java SE 11 Programmer Exam:

The **1Z0-815:Java Exam** certification is an internationally-recognized certification which help to have validation for those professionals who are keen to make their career in Java Technology.

This exam aspirant are accustomed to the ideas and therefore the concepts of Java Technology . Candidates should have some hands-on experience with Declare, instantiate one dimensional array, applying encapsulation and understanding lambda expressions. These candidates can go for this exam.

- Fresher
- IT coder / developer

How to study the 1Z0-815:Java SE 11 Programmer Exam:

Preparation of certification exams could be covered with two resource types . The first one are the study guides, reference books and study forums that are elaborated and appropriate for building information from ground up. Apart from them video tutorials and lectures are a good option to ease the pain of through study and are relatively make the study process more interesting nonetheless these demand time and concentration from the learner. Smart candidates who wish to create a solid foundation altogether examination topics and connected technologies typically mix video lectures with study guides to reap the advantages of each but practice exams or practice exam engines is one important study tool which goes typically unnoted by most candidates. Practice exams are designed with our experts to make exam prospects test their knowledge on skills attained in course, as well as prospects become comfortable and familiar with the real exam environment. Statistics have indicated exam anxiety plays much bigger role of students failure in exam than the fear of the unknown. Certification-questions expert team recommends preparing some notes on these topics along with it don't forget to practice **1Z0-815:Java dumps** which had been written by our expert team, each of these can assist you loads to clear this exam with excellent marks.

1Z0-815:Java SE 11 Programmer Exam Certification Path:

1Z0-815:Java SE 11 Programmer Exam is foundation level Certification.
As such There is no prerequisite for this course. Anyone who is having keen and familiar with Java technology are well invited to pursue this certification.

How much Java Windows Server Fundamentals Exam Cost:

The price of the Java Windows Server Fundamentals exam is $245 USD, for more information related to exam price please visit to Java Training website as prices of Java exams fees get varied country wise.

How to book the 1Z0-815:Java SE 11 Programmer Exam:

Purchase an exam voucher now and redeem it within 6 months. These are following steps for registering the 1Z0-815:Java SE 11

Programmer exam.

- Step 1: Visit to Java Learning and search for 1Z0-815:Java SE 11 Programmer
- Step 2: Sign up/Login to Pearson VUE account
- Step 3: Select local centre based on your country, date, time and confirm with a payment method.

What is the duration, language, and format of 1Z0-815:Java SE 11 Programmer Exam:

- Length of Examination: 180 mins
- Number of Questions: 80
- Passing Score 63%
- Type of Questions: This test format is multiple choice.
- language: English

1Z0-815:Java SE 11 Programmer Exam Certified Professional salary:

The average salary of a 1Z0-815:Java SE 11 Programmer Exam Certified Expert in

- United State - 134,247 USD
- India - 17,20,327 INR
- Europe - 88,547 EURO
- England - 78,632 POUND

The benefit of obtaining the 1Z0-815:Java SE 11 Programmer Exam Certification:

- 1Z0-815:Java Certification is distinguished among competitors. 1Z0-815:Java certification can give them an edge at that time easily when candidates appear for employment interview, employers are very fascinated to note one thing that differentiates the individual from all other candidates.

- 1Z0-815:Java certification has more useful and relevant networks that help them in setting career goals for themselves. 1Z0-815:Java networks provide them with the correct career guidance than non certified generally are unable to get.
- 1Z0-815:Java will be confident and stand different from others as their skills are more trained than non-certified professionals.
- **1Z0-815:Java Exam** provide proven knowledge to use the tools to complete the task efficiently and cost effectively than the other non-certified professionals lack in doing so.
- 1Z0-815:Java Certification provides practical experience to candidates from all the aspects to be a proficient worker in the organization.
- 1Z0-815:Java Certifications provide opportunities to get a job easily in which they are interested in instead of wasting years and ending without getting any experience.

Difficulty in Writing 1Z0-815:Java SE 11 Programmer Exam:

Candidates face many problems when they start preparing for the 1Z0-815:Java SE 11 Programmer. These Certification may go tough for those participants who are not prepared enough. If a candidate wants to prepare himself for the 1Z0-815:Java SE 11 Programmer without any problem and get good grades in the exam, Then candidates should show their dedication in learning about this certification. Apart from that by choosing the best real exam questions practice you will manage to get through with this certification. There are many websites that are offering the latest 1Z0-815:Java SE 11 Programmer questions and answers but these questions are not verified by Google certified experts and that's why many are failed in their just first attempt.

Certification-questions is the best platform which provides the candidate with the necessary 1Z0-815 Java Exam questions that will help him to pass the 1Z0-815:Java SE 11 Programmer on the first time. Candidate will not have to take the 1Z0-815:Java SE 11 Programmer twice because with the help of **1Z0-815 Java dumps** Candidate will have every valuable material required to pass the Google 1Z0-815:Java SE 11 Programmer. We are providing the latest and actual questions and that is the reason why this is the one that he needs to use and there are no chances to fail when a candidate will have valid dumps from Certification-questions. We have the guarantee that the questions that we have will be the ones that will pass candidate in the 1Z0-815:Java SE 11 Programmer in the very first attempt.

For more info read reference::

Java learning site
Java Programming Learning Subscription
Core Java Learning Subscription

Sample Practice Test for 1Z0-815

Question: 1 *One Answer Is Right*

Given:

```java
public class A {
  private boolean checkValue(int val) {
    return true;
  }
}
```

and

```java
public class B extends A {
  public int modifyVal(int val) {
    if(checkValue(val)) {
      return val;
    } else {
      return 0;
    }
  }
  public static void Main(String[] args) {
    B b = new B();
    System.out.println(b.modifyVal(10));
  }
}
```

What is the result?

Answers:

A) nothing

B) It fails to compile.

C) 0

D) A java.lang.IllegalArgumentException is thrown.

E) 10

Solution: B

Explanation:

Explanation:

```java
public class A {
    private boolean checkValue(int val) {
        return true;
    }
}
and
public class B extends A {
    public int modifyVal(int val) {
        if(checkValue(val)) {
            return val;
        } else {
            return 0;
        }
    }
    public static void Main(String[] args) {
        B b = new B();
        system.out.println(b.modfiyVal (10));
    }
}
```

Execute Mode, Version, Inputs & Arguments

JDK 11.0.4

CommandLine Arguments

Result
CPU Time: sec(s), Memory: kilobyte(s)

```
/A.java:6: error: class, interface, or enum expected
and
^
1 error
```

Question: 2 *One Answer Is Right*

Given:
```
public interface API {    //line 1
  public void checkValue(Object value)
             throws IllegalArgumentException; //line 2
  public boolean isValueANumber(Object val) {
    if(val instanceof Number) {
      return true;
    }else {
      try {
         Double.parseDouble(val.toString());
         return true;
      }catch (NumberFormatException ex) {
        return false;
      }
    }
  }
}
```

Which two changes need to be made to make this class compile? (Choose two.)

Answers:

A) Change Line 1 to an abstract class: public abstract class API {

B) Change Line 2 access modifier to protected: protected void checkValue(Object value) throws IllegalArgumentException;

C) Change Line 1 to a class: public class API {

D) Change Line 1 to extend java.lang.AutoCloseable: public interface API extends AutoCloseable {

E) Change Line 2 to an abstract method: public abstract void checkValue(Object value) throws IllegalArgumentException;

Solution: C, E

Question: 3 *One Answer Is Right*

Which two modules include APIs in the Java SE Specification? (Choose two.)

Answers:

A) java.logging

B) java.desktop

C) javafx

D) jdk.httpserver

E) jdk.jartool

Solution: A, D

Explanation:

Explanation: Reference:
https://docs.oracle.com/javase/9/docs/api/overview-summary.html

Question: 4 *One Answer Is Right*

Given:
```
public class Test{
    private int num = 1;
    private int div = 0;

    public void divide() {
        try {
            num = num / div;
            System.out.print("Exception");
        }
        catch(ArithmeticException ae) { num = 100; }
        catch(Exception e) { num = 200; }
        finally { num = 300; }
        System.out.print(num);
    }
    public static void main(String args[])
    {
        Test test = new Test();
        test.divide();
    }
}
```
What is the output?

Answers:

A) 300

B) Exception

C) 200

D) 100

Solution: A

Explanation:

Explanation:

```java
public class Test{
    private int num = 1;
    private int div = 0;

    public void divide() {
        try {
            num = num / div;
            System.out.print("Exception");
        }
        catch(ArithmeticException ae) { num = 100; }
        catch(Exception e) { num = 200; }
        finally { num = 300; }
        System.out.print(num);
    }
    public static void main(String args[])
    {
        Test test = new Test();
        test.divide();
    }
}
```

Execute Mode, Version, Inputs & Arguments

JDK 11.0.4

CommandLine Arguments

Result
CPU Time: 0.15 sec(s), Memory: 32484 kilobyte(s)

300

Question: 5 *One Answer Is Right*

Which two statements are true about the modular JDK? (Choose two.)

Answers:

A) The foundational APIs of the Java SE Platform are found in the java.base module.

B) An application must be structured as modules in order to run on the modular JDK.

C) It is possible but undesirable to configure modules' exports from the command line.

D) APIs are deprecated more aggressively because the JDK has been modularized.

Solution: A, B

Question: 6 *One Answer Is Right*

Given the code fragment:
```
int[] secA = { 2, 4, 6, 8, 10 };
int[] secB = { 2, 4, 8, 6, 10 };
int res1 = Arrays.mismatch(secA, secB);
int res2 = Arrays.compare(secA, secB);
System.out.print(res1 + " : " + res2);
```
What is the result?

Answers:

A) -1 : 2

B) 2 : -1

C) 2 : 3

D) 3 : 0

Solution: A

Question: 7 *One Answer Is Right*

Given:

```java
import java.io.*;
public class Tester {
   public static void main(String[] args) {
      try {
         doA();
         doB();
      } catch(IOException e) {
         System.out.print("c");
         return;
      } finally{
         System.out.print("d");
      }
      System.out.print("f");
   }
   private static void doA() {
      System.out.print("a");
      if (false) {
         throw new IndexOutOfBoundsException();
      }
   }
   private static void doB() throws FileNotFoundException {
      System.out.print("b");
      if (true) {
         throw new FileNotFoundException();
      }
   }
}
```

What is the result?

Answers:

A) The compilation fails.

B) abdf

C) abd

D) adf

E) abcd

Solution: A

Question: 8 *One Answer Is Right*

Which set of commands is necessary to create and run a custom runtime image from Java source files?

Answers:

A) java, jdeps

B) javac, jlink

C) jar, jlink

D) javac, jar

Solution: C

Explanation:

Explanation: Reference:
https://blogs.oracle.com/jtc/automating-the-creation-of-jdk9-reduced-runtime-images-in- netbeans

Question: 9 *One Answer Is Right*

Given:
```
public class Tester {
    public static void main(String[] args) {
        StringBuilder sb = new StringBuilder(5);
        sb.append("HOWDY");
        sb.insert(0, ' ');
        sb.replace(3, 5, "LL");
        sb.insert(6, "COW");
        sb.delete(2, 7);
        System.out.println(sb.length());
    }
}
```
What is the result?

Answers:

A) 4

B) 3

C) An exception is thrown at runtime.

D) 5

Solution: D

Explanation:

Explanation:

```
 6  public class Tester {
 7      public static void main(String[] args) {
 8          StringBuilder sb = new StringBuilder (5);
 9          sb.append ("HOWDY") ;
10          sb.insert (0, ' ');
11          sb.replace(3, 5, "LL");
12          sb.insert (6, "^COW");
13          sb.delete(2, 7);
14          System.out.println(sb.length());
15      }
16  }
```

(command line arguments)

| COMPILE & EXECUTE | PASTE SOURCE |

Successfully compiled /tmp/java_82Tlan/Tester.java <-- main method   5

Question: 10 *One Answer Is Right*

Given:

```
import java.util.function.BiFunction;
public class Pair<T> {
    final BiFunction<T, T, Boolean> validator;
    T left = null;
    T right = null;
    private Pair() {
      validator=null;
    }
    Pair(BiFunction<T, T, Boolean> v, T x, T y) {
        validator = v;
        set(x, y);
    }
    void set(T x, T y) {
        if (!validator.apply(x, y)) throw new IllegalArgumentException();
        setLeft(x);
        setRight(y);
    }
    void setLeft(T x) {
        left = x;
    }
    void setRight(T y) {
        right = y;
    }
    final boolean isValid() {
        return validator.apply(left, right);
    }
}
```

It is required that if p instanceof Pair then p.isValid() returns true. Which is the smallest set of visibility changes to insure this requirement is met?

Answers:

A) setLeft and setRight must be protected.

B) left and right must be private.

C) isValid must be public.

D) left, right, setLeft, and setRight must be private.

Solution: B

SUMMARY

To recap, main stages of certification exam study guide are Introduction to Java Exam , Java Exam topics in which Candidates must know the exam topics before they start of preparation, Java Exam Requirements, Cost of Java Exam, registration procedure of the Java Exam, Java Exam formate, Java Exam Certified salary, JavaExam advantages.

If you are aspirant to pass the cerification exam, start exam preparation with study material provided by Certification-questions.com

About The Author

David Mayer

Co-Founder of Certification-Questions.com

David is the Co-founder of Certification-Questions.com, one of the largest Certification practice tests and PDF exams websites on the Internet. They are providing dumps an innovative way by providing Online Web Simulator and Mobile App. He likes to share his knowledge and is active in the Java community.

He has written several books, blogs, and is active in the Java community.

APPENDIX

Certification

The action or process of providing someone or something with an official document that accredits a state or level of results.

Practice test

The practical exam is an alternative, non-scoring version of the intermediate or final exam of the course. The practice exam has the same format as the "real" exam, which means that if the practice exam has 20 multiple-choice questions and four free-answer questions, the "real" exam will be the same.

CPSIA information can be obtained
at www.ICGtesting.com
Printed in the USA
LVHW022157140121
676498LV00028B/875